:boys

Poems

Luke Johnson

BLUE HORSE PRESS REDONDO BEACH, CALIFORNIA 2019

:boys

Luke Johnson

Blue Horse Press
318 Avenue I # 760
Redondo Beach,
California   90277

Cover photo: "Haunting the Backroads of Missouri."
Justin Hamm ©
Used by permission

Editors: Jeffrey and Tobi Alfier
Blue Horse Press logo: Amy Lynn Hayes (1996)

ISBN 978-0-578-49632-0

FIRST EDITION © 2019

This and other Blue Horse Press Titles may be found at
www.bluehorsepress.com

For Giana, Malakai & Micah. For Smitty, too.

Acknowledgements

Much thanks to the following journals where some of these poems appeared, sometimes in different versions:

American Journal of Poetry, "Rats & Manna"

Asheville Poetry Review, ":boys" (formerly under the title "Boys")

Connotation Press, "Deadwind" and "Witchery"

Cultural Weekly, "Beetroot" and "Hum"

Greensboro Review, "WTR"

Isacoustic, ":boys" (reprinted and formerly under the title "Boys")

Kenyon Review, "I'll talk sadness, sure"

Narrative, "Finch"

Nimrod, "Song of the Stillborn"

Porter Gulch Review, "Bee Fennel"

Misfit.net, "Like a Fish Gasping"

Tilde, "Malakai" (formerly under the title, "Messenger")

Tinderbox, "Numbers 14:18"

The Lake, "WTR" (reprinted)

"Finch" was featured as Poem of the Week with *Narrative*, October 2018.

"Song of the Stillborn" was a finalist for the Pablo Neruda Award.

"Numbers 14:18" was a finalist for the Brett Elizabeth Jenkins Awar

"Hum" was nominated for Best of the Net.

"Malakai" (formerly titled "Messenger") was nominated for a Pushcart.

Writing poetry is an often confounding, isolating task. Thank you to the following people for investing in me as a poet: Ciara, my wife. You were the first to tell me I could actually do this. My children: Giana, Malakai and Micah. You three are my greatest muse. My mom Corinne, and sisters: Camille and Melaine. Thank you for loving me into the poet I am. Patricia Smith, for your unyielding push and presence in these lines. Brian Turner, Lee Herrick, Laura McCullough, and all the wonderful SNC faculty. Kathryn Delancellotti and Samuel Duarte, for true friendship in and outside poetry. Jeff and Tobi Alfier, for your keen interest in me and my work. Jordan Rice, Dexter L. Booth, Pat Salisbury, Andrew McFayden-Ketchum, Laure-Anne Bosselaar, Timothy Liu, Alexis Rhone Fancher, Kai Carlson-Wee, Ivan Brownotter, Max Heinegg, Francesca Bell, Kelly Michels, Luke Hankins, Jenn Givhan, Michael Schmeltzer, Joe Amaral, Kevin Patrick Sullivan, James Cushing, Connie Post, Cameron Lawrence, David Sullivan, Michael LaRonn, Geri Lucas, Shaneen Harris, Katy Day, Faylita Hicks, and many, many more!

Contents

"I am here, in my father's house.
I who am half of your world…"
James Dickey

:boys

– to Smitty, Slick Nic, Mortimer and Dave

In a barn
choked by rusty tools
and ragweed

we stood
in a riotous circle

watching
fetal mice fill
their fresh lungs with air

when Smitty
behind a tribal smile

pulled a blade
from his back pocket

and began
to slice one down the abdomen
with ball point precision

each of us stone-silent
and cold

as Smitty unsnapped
the sternum
    like a bloody brassiere

then moved toward
the heart

a porous drum
swelling in his fingers.

Numbers 14:18

I've never told you
how my father tied
a drunk man to a chair

and snapped the first four fingers
on his left hand.

How the moon,
a sickle soaked in milk
hung center the window
cracked from frantic birds

and how the man, his dad,
howled like a stray in the hills
the boys bragged of maiming.

You might be wondering
what happened to the fifth finger
his thumb

and whether it stayed straight
or faced a similar form of fracture.

But none of that matters.

In the time it'd take
to detail a thumb pried loose, I

could move from the shed
to the house
a quarter mile north,

where my nana
swirls thyme in soup

and sways her hips
to Stevie Wonder, John Prine.

How can she dance
when the dead crawl inside?

How can she dance
with a body branded,
owned by a beast, a belt
that blooms the tremors?

Believe when I tell you
the fifth was spared.

That my father
ran out of whisky,
out of spite,

stopped soothing with blood
sought light

and stepped out
deeply hidden, an animal
crazed for water.

That he found in his search
an oasis

and there
lapped stars until shame clotted
concealed

spread like yeast
and swallowed him.

Sometimes that's all
that it takes. One taste.
One. For deadwind

to enter and eat
the insides

of a boy of a boy of a boy
of a boy of a boy of a boy
                    of a boy—

Beetroot

Here is where an umbilical budded
like a beetroot. Where my drunk

daddy cut the cord crooked, left

a piece like frayed shoestring. If
you put an ear to it, you can hear

tentacles slip inside ribs, consume

me. Now squint as if looking through
a peephole. Notice a moon-shaped

mark marred by a smoke-butt. I

found pleasure there. I let the cat
lick it clean.

WTR
to Dad, Uncle K, Fred and a few others

My father
flips flapjacks
from a gas grill,

while a few
of his friends

pass a joint
and bullshit stories
from the seventies.

I'm sitting
by the remains
of last night's fire,

listening to
smoldering mesquite
crawl deeper into dirt

its sizzle
like the grill

as it spits
and pops batter back
from dad's fingers.

Every so often
I rummage
through ruins
of charred bark

to rediscover
a blue flame
riffing like a flag.

I hover my hand
above it,
smile

as a blister
forms to an island
in the center of a scar.

Dad dances plates
of eggs and flapjacks
to the table,

rocking hillbilly hips
to Clapton's contagious solo.

He says: Come sit son,
here, by me, my beautiful boy,

moving a wrinkled
stack of Playboys
and a few bottles of Beam.

I rise to my feet
like *white trash royalty*,
demand they serve me my meal.

Deadwind

after Kai Carlson-Wee

There must be sea, gunmetal sky.

There must be gulls plucking flesh

from beached seals

and carrying carcass to their young.

A drunk woman stumbling in head high surf.

There must be kite string snapping

when the line let's out.

A boy's cry. A mother's sobering concern.

A father from a distance with a cigarette.

One hand strangling the neck of a bottle,

the other rested flat on a dog with skin disease.

There must be a black umbrella, always an umbrella,

even when it's warm an umbrella, a feeling like an umbrella,

a sadness like sand in the gums.

There must be fallen palms, bark stripped clean

by homeless. Burn barrels. Braided smoke. A fight.

A drunk woman stumbling in head high surf.

A father from a distance with a cigarette,

one hand strangling a neck.

There must be a moon red sickled

and a wind that deadens, the way breath deadens,

when choked with ash, so much falling ash.

And this boy, desperate boy.

Charting a route from here, to someplace in heaven.

Liner Notes to Benjamin

Most nights our mother
makes a gesture while she sleeps:

one hand balled in a fist,
while the other slaps the headboard
and she chokes.

—

Too many times
she's strolled a snowy dark
with eyes rolled back in her head.

Balanced a bridge rail
to tempt the wind —
mocking the body's balance.

—

Brother, come.

Spread snow along the floor
and shape your feet in little indentations.

I'll follow you into the fields.

–

When I hold my breath
an inch under bathwater,

you crouch by the sink
with a bird in your teeth,
both eyes puddled and stark.

Why do you smile
when I speak your name,

spin from my whispers, and fade?
–

Forgive the times
I begged
because the wine was gone

and her hands began
to itch,

because I could not
carry your name.

All she wished
was to touch your lips,

turn their tarnish to feathers.

13

—

We have these mittens:

booties woven blue
with lace like silken pearls

and this photo:

dad bearded,
both hands pressed to her belly:

      one black kite
      in a sky beginning
      to smear.

Witchery

I wore the white batik and flat sandals
and walked the jungle road

looking for the pillar with the bell.
I happened upon a blind woman

throating guttural
like my friend Jonah that night at church

when his jaw unlocked
and eyes rolled back

and every evil snapped inside
his barreled chest

causing his voice to froth and throb
and sinew fat blue and veiny

like the woman begging the invisible
to twist out from gypsum sand

and braille along the bamboo floor
a warning about my future:

No go here. You, no go.
Winds do bad things.

Ramda come clicking
from sugar cane,

howl inside your blood.
Give me money Luke

though I never told her my name.

Bee Fennel

I trapped bees in boxes
and carried them to the neighbor's blind son.

Set them loose. Praised their frantic undulations,
their search for someone to serve,

then left him, bitten, tongue partly swollen,
stomach distended and scabbed. Edit: I did not

simply set them free in the blind boy's hair. I
wooed them with candy and blew smoke through

a hole in the box until they dropped dizzy.
Plucked their stingers. Drowned the queen

and smiled as her wings folded into soda pop.
Promised the boy a taste of fennel, hot joy

thrumming his throat. He opened. Teeth
clean. Teeth like washed windows. Tasted

my kiss. Unraveled my tongue inside his.

Like a Fish Gasping

Did I tell you a boy was walking home from school,
when a woman asked him if he'd like a cup of juice?

Did I tell you Jonah heard his mother's voice
and muted her concern?

Did I tell you the woman grew angry, began
to weep, threatened to follow him home?

Did I tell you Jonah ran?

Did I tell you she set her three dogs free to harm him?

Did I tell you Jonah found his home, but the back door
was locked?

Did I tell you Jonah ran?

Did I tell you Jonah never said no, that he found her offer
kind, and besides, she was an elderly woman anyway?

Did I tell you the home was large with locked windows,
no dogs?

Did I tell you Jonah sat down, his brow was warm,
he needed just a sip?

Did I tell you he had more than a sip?

Did I tell you as he drank his body began to wobble,
he fell, that he dreamed of fish fondled by blades?

Did I tell you he woke with bloody fingers?

Did I tell you he was my friend, he loved fingers,
that he liked to suck fingers?

Did I tell you Jonah ran?

Did I tell you he woke with his pants undone
and a broom stick up his ass?

Did I tell you Jonah liked fingers?

I offered my fingers, found pleasure, strange
pleasure, felt shame, I silenced the Lord.

Did I tell you I silenced the Lord?

Did I tell you I woke with a sheet over my mouth
and Jonah began to piss?

Did I tell you I swallowed piss?

I gasped like a fish out of waves.

Did I tell you I swallowed piss?

Did I tell you Jonah ran, never came home, his body
a house without windows?

Did I tell you Jonah ran?

Did I tell you he put a gun to his head and did what the whispers wanted?

Did I tell you it wasn't his fault?

Hum

An El Camino
bumps Beastie Boys
in a parking garage,

when two
broad shouldered dudes
emerge from dumpster fire

and lumber
like vagrant shadows.

They jab
each other's ribs   talk shit,

boast about the pussy
they'll crush later at the L,

then laugh
while bagging a beer.

> The man in the car
> is my dad's friend Jake.
>
> He's high on hash
> and learning to cope

                                    with flashbacks
                              of boys blown open —
                          insides scattered by birds.

                                 Jake doesn't know
                          now is the moment he'll die

                                 the moment a gun
                          he's shined from boyhood

                          will erase puddled light
                              and spill it like silk
                                    from his lips.

He pulls the pistol
from the front dash,
spins its chamber,

glides blurred vision
down the gun's oil slicked
exterior, snaps it shut.

Scans the boys.
Frames their faces
as they approach the car quietly.

One taps the window,
while the other draws a light.

How much you need?

22

All you got, he says,

flashing back to the first
buck he narrowed
through a scope as a boy.

How the crowned beast
wobbled jack-lit pine
like a lopped ballerina,

how he held it under
'til the kicking stopped.

Lice & Feathers

Chloe's booties
left unfinished & kept in plastic
in a box beneath the shed.

When alone, I'd
wear them on my thumbs

& imagine her heels first wobble
then the want to run away.

//

Months our mother
gnawed her tongue & spit pieces of it

into day old glasses of water.
They'd float like fetal tissue

then stick to the glasses like warts.

///

Priests prayed
& doctors mocked their prayers,
offered pills:

one white tablet
after each sudden tremor.

////

Twice I heard a baby wail
in the wall behind my bed.

/////

Twice my mother bound my mouth,
blew smoke inside my nose.

//////

I'd dig until my nails were gone,
her wail a drowned violin.

//////

She'd pick until her skin was scarred,
looking for lice & feathers.

Jonah Revisited

I never told them
my name. The fists beating

bruises under Jonah's sculpted
stomach. And yet they drew me close

to kiss his navel   cries
                a hapless crane —

I'll talk sadness, sure,

after Brandon Melendez

but not about my sister
alone in a closet
with a mouse & book
of matches. So, here
is a pick & pane of ice
to stab until the pond spills.
Here is daddy's cane
frayed from blunt force
& its serpentine slap.
Here is the cat kicked
crooked for clawing
mother's wrist. A Remi.
Brass knuckles. Silk
blouse rutted by moths.
Here is a fence post
snapped to a spear.
A rope. Sticky needle.
A tulip chewed into pulp.
And laughter, as if it
were lodged in a drain.
Drowned, knotted with hair.

Rats & Manna

This poem has a house on a slipped foundation
and a woman beneath the porch
with a wrench

trying to tie down the posts. She's heavy-set
with small hands
and bites her lips until they bleed.

Above her
footsteps thud and dust swarms. She admires
the way the refraction of light comes close

and whorls when her hand moves through it.
Remembers her father preaching and pacing
the aisles between pews

while her silent mother
flipped a black bible and wrote notes,
gin on her breath. These days all it takes

is a gentle gale to shake the house.
If you're standing by the stove frying tilapia
and a storm congeals

and what follows that storm
are silk howls wrapped with rain, you'll feel
your feet wobble

as the structure cracks like ship boughs,
shifts for balance. This is a poem more
than a house. A poem about a woman

who fixes three plates for supper,
who waits patiently for the back door
to hook and close

and the house to erupt with laughter so loud
the wood shutters slap, metal sconces shake.
But there are no footsteps here,

no voices in the clearing,
no lover's hand moving the hair from her face
when she fights fever or builds a fence

or ties down the house
so, the earth won't swallow her.
This is a poem about prayer, about the loss of prayer,

about rats who nest inside walls and leave shit
lined from room to room like manna. About two
plates left like offerings, for a lover and son

she carried six months into light.

Hypnos

I hear
a hundred yards from home
a call   someone calling

a cry mistook for a loon
on a lake   lake lapping

beached oars swishing
where tide shores.

I hear
and make in my hearing a boy
boy on a dock

swilling his face
from the lake's glassed surface
with a stick sheared off by a hand saw.

The boy is hungry.
I know this by the way a stone slackens
in the cleft of his palm

as it tilts before sinking
to eelgrass.

Soon it will rain.
And the boy who is nobody's son

who ran from sky
with snake and bread
and a body torn by dogs

will build a fire
and blind his eyes with soot.

He will live inside dreams
in search of wings that are lost.

Malakai

I would not name Him,
could not cut the throbbing umbilical,

nor listen to him suckle, small calf,
then coo a reckoning, contusions
like clusters of stars.

Song of the Stillborn

i.

I lifted a calf from a barn floor
and despite its mother's refusal
left it for the pigs. They would not gather, no,

would not come from their pens
to feed from what had been offered.

The cord was wrapped around the still-dripping calf,
tongue unraveled, torso spotted with vernix.

I could have bound rocks to its ankles
and trusted it to tumble into boulders, break open,
become food for bottom feeders.

I could have built a fire, body lifted by smoke.

I did neither, no, I fit it back into the warmth
of its mother's mucus, and rested its chin
on her swollen belly. I could have cut a seam
in the belly of that dead calf

and placed the cut to the mother's nipple
as if it would could come alive there and feed.

ii.

That Summer my son was putty in my hands.
He came from brackish waters,

eyes nested with terror. He came
as one comes wailing from resurrection.

I lifted him from my lover's breasts
and despite the voice inside me saying run
don't ever look back, prophesied prosperity,

likened his hunger with mine. Bit him by the heart
and smoothed the impression into a seamless dimple.

Reader believe me:
I did not take the mother in the holler
and put a bullet through her brain. She was no

longer milkable, yes, and her calf left
for the buzzards, yes,

but there's something beautiful about a body
picked down to its spine.

> How it carries its shape.
> How it softens over time.

Finch

i.

My son swats a finch with his bat
and laughs

when my daughter swoops
the breathing bird in her arms

and runs toward the river.
There, she stitches

the bird's torn wing with staples
and hangs it to a tree. All day

she speaks
as if she's never noticed its shadow

swaying above the chanterelles.

ii.

I read of a boy in Birmingham
who set fire to barns along an empty interstate.

He trapped horses in stalls
and admitted, when questioned,

It wasn't the thought of the roof imploding,
but the flurry of ash thereafter.

iii.

I want to tell you
how my daughter

laid the bird in a wood box
and dropped a match.

How she wept
as it wings went up in smoke.

But bear with me.

A little girl's sorrow
is worth a hundred men's lives.

iv.

Sometimes, on a walk,
looking for butterflies or fallen fruit,

I'll send my son a few hundred feet
to scout,

and ask, when he returns,
whether the acreage up ahead

is worthwhile. If so,
we'll eat until our stomachs ache. If not,

I'll demand he go a little farther,
looking for fruit

without bruised ruts or flies, finch
in the foreground singing.

v.

Last summer
a wildfire gnawed spruce
to snapping tinder. Silence lumbered

the sky's carved dome
and came closer. At night it swelled
the blurred interior

like a lung of light. I'd wait
by the window, watching, wait
until sunrise. Listen for sounds

of my son's feet
racing across the cloven field, forbid
him to pass through the gate.

About the Author

Luke James Johnson was born and raised on the California coast. When he isn't vacuuming or chasing kids, he spends his time writing. He lives in California with his wife, three children and bluepoint Siamese cat named Louie. His poems may be found in *Kenyon Review*, *Florida Review*, *Narrative Magazine*, *Nimrod*, *Tinderbox*, *The Asheville Poetry Review*, *Greensboro Review*, *The American Journal of Poetry* and *Connotation Press* among others. His poem, "Messenger", was nominated for the Pushcart Prize by *Tilde*, and *Hum* was nominated "Best of the Net" by *Cultural Weekly*. His work was also a finalist for The Pablo Neruda Prize and The Brett Elizabeth Jenkins Award. He completed his MFA in Creative Writing at Sierra Nevada College.